INTRODUCTION

Start your daily activities with this life inspirational book. In the symphony of life, these carefully crafted words are ready to become your daily companion—concise and full of wisdom. Each quote is based on life experience and not a theory.

Each quote serves as a guiding light to illuminate your life path with insight and motivation. From the deep reflections of ancient philosophers to the contemporary whispers of modern thinkers, this collection invites you to understand life better.

Finally, enjoy reading this book where simplicity and wisdom merge in the art of everyday life. Happy reading and if you enjoy it please consider leaving a review.

Robbert Piontek

you called it "being alone"
I call it "enjoying my own company"

"focus on the goal don't get distracted"

" The crazy thing about people
who don't like you,
they watch everything you do "

" once I hug the pillow,
there is a 95 percent chance
I will fail to achieve my goal."

"I looked at my mother when someone
asked me about unconditional love"

" don't lose hope
when the sun sets the star comes out "

" Always do what is right not what is good "

" don't look for a happy life, make it happens."

" People leave you out in the cold
but they get mad when you know
how to warm yourself "

" You become very dangerous person
once you learn how to control your feelings "

" I don't care who is better than me
I am just doing better than I was yesterday,
I am my real competitor "

" I don't chase,
what belongs to me will come to me
soon or later "

" Love what you have
before life teaches you to love what you lost "

" if you choose money over love
you always be poor "

" being able to breathe for 1 whole year
is a miracle. be aware and use your time
to be grateful "

" the worst prison in the world
is a home without peace "

" It's my turn to be happy "

" At the end love will always win "

" People who never loved will move on easily "

"When your intention was pure
you will not lose anything,
but they will"

"If you didn't fight for what you want
don't cry for it."

"Sometimes you have to suffer in this life
not because you were bad,
but because you didn't know when to stop
being good"

"When you destroy someone's life with lies,
take it as a loan, it will come back to you
with its interest"

"Sometimes the best thing you can find
when you keep your mouth shut and
keep your eyes open. The truth will come out"

"The worst time of your life is when you can see the true color of everyone"

*"If my words can not change you
then my silence will"*

*"Don't judge people
you don't know what they have survived
so far"*

"Love is given, not asked"

*"Your degree is just a piece of paper
your education is seen in your behavior"*

*"Your value is not seen until
your absence is felt"*

*"If I can not trust you
I don't need you."*

"You become what you believe"

"When it is easy for you,
watch your steps"

"Not every close door is locked,
open it !"

"Stay away from idiots,
no need to waste your time
arguing with them"

"Hate is heavy, Let it go"

*"Solve the problem or leave it,
don't stay with it"*

"Find your own peace"

*"A single lie is enough to create doubt
in every single truth"*

*"Never ignore the sign you asked GOD
to show you"*

"Respect the old when you are young, help
the weak when you are strong, confess
your faults when you're wrong"
because one day, you will be
old, weak and wrong."

"Everything will come to you
at the right time"

"Monster doesn't sleep under you bed,
It stays inside your head"

"If it is important to you,
Find a way !"

"Lies travel faster than truth."

"Never make a decision based on
temporary emotion."

"You will never make it
if you care about what others think."

"Don't let your feelings get to deep
people change anytime"

"Slow succes build character,
fast success build ego"

"Be yourself,
people don't have to like you
and you dont't have to care."

"Some people want to see you fail
disappoint them !"

"When your heart breaks,
your brain starts working"

*"Nobody is coming to save you,
Get up"*

*"Your character is about who you are,
your reputation is about what people think
about what you are"*

"Don't be affraid to start over again"

"Always start with what you have"

"Focus on process not result"

*"Don't think about yesterday,
think about now and tomorrow."*

*"Don't say happy new year if
you don't care about the whole year."*

"Don't wait , create your own way."

"Always do what you are affraid to do."

*"Once you learn how to create
your own happiness
no one can take it from you."*

*"You can have the worst day in your life,
but few weeks later you have the best day.
So keep pushing through."*

*"The past is behind, learn from it.
The future is ahead, prepare for it.
the present is here, live it.*

"Be happy is not because everything
is good, but because you can see
the positive side of everything."

"Never give up,
today is hard, tomorrow will be worst
but the day after tomorrow will be sunshine."

"When people smile all the time, it doesn't
mean their life is perfect. Their smile symbolized
hope and strength."

"Fortune helps the brave."

"Be an eagle, silence and it can touch
the sky."

"Only you can change the situation
Don't hope other people to do it"

"Don't waste your time to impress people
around you. You will be tired"

"No matter how hard your life is,
keep fighting."

"If we could spread love as quickly as
we spread hate and negativity, what amazing
world we live in."

"There will be always haters,
the more you grow, the more they hate.
so, keep going."

"Good things take time."

"Use everyday as an opportunity
to make tomorrow even more better"

"Don't give up,
the beginning is always the hardest."

"Never forget where you come from
never lose sight where you are going to."

'Never lose hope, today is worse
but tomorrow could be the day
you are waiting for."

"once you start to belive in yourself
miracle starts happening."

*"Don't think too much,
just do it."*

*"Focus on solution not on problem,
don't waste time worrying too much."*

*"Take a risk, If win you will be happy,
if lose you will be wise."*

*"Motivate yourself, don't listen to
those people who only see
your mistake ."*

"True happines based on
your own peace."

"Don't stay somewhere you are not
valued and appreciated"

"happiness is not about getting all
you want, it is about enjoying
what you have."

'Never tell anyone your plan,
show them the result instead"

"My life , my own rules"

'Don't let other people's behaviors
destroy your peace."

"Change your attitude, mindset and
actions consistently. "Something"
will come to you"

"Life is short, use it wisely."

"Stop being affraid of the space
between your dream and reality
remember, if you can dream it,
you can achieve it."

"as long as you are breathing,
everything is possible, never quit trying
make the rest of your life becomes the best."

"Never react on every situation,
stop being emotional all the time."

"As long as you keep trying
there is still hope."

"Tell yourself : today is my day."

"An arrow only can be shot by pulling it
backward. When life is dragging you back
with difficulties. It means, it is going to
launch you into something great.
Focus and keep aiming"

"Forget who hurts you but
remember who loves
you every single day"

"They see failure, I see lesson."

"Accept the facts that everyone
will leave you even people who promised
to stay."

"Be good enough to forgive people,
but don't be stupid to trust them
again."

"Sometimes you don't need to hear
their excuses, their actions already
spoke the truth."

"Don't beg anyone to stay
Your goal is more important."

"don't get distracted by something
that has nothing to do with your goal"

"A goal without actions is just a wish."

'Wise men solve the problem,
but idiots find an excuse"

"Only the strong survive"

"Be careful what you tell people,
A friend today could be an enemy
tomorrow"

"Every problem is gift,
without it, we can not grow."

"Speak less and open your eyes"

"People always come and leave
in your life, but the right one
will stay."

*"If you are affraid of failure
you don't deserve to be
successful"*

*"Do everything with good heart
and expect nothing in return and you
will be never disappointed."*

*"Two things define you, your patience
when you have nothing, your attitude
when you have everything."*

*"Trust your instincts,
it knows when it's time to
walk away."*

"Respect people who tell you the truth,
no matter how bad it is."

"Everyone has their own time,
Be patience."

"Be careful how much you tolerate it,
you are teaching them how to
treat you."

"Your mindset determines
the quality of your life."

"in due time
the real will be separated from
the fake."

Önce you become fearless
your strength become limitless"

"Once you feel avoided by someone
don't disturb them again."

"Never feel sad about losing anything,
When a tree loses its leaves, new leaves
will show up."

*"There is huge freedom
when you take nothing personally."*

*"Sometimes you will never know
the value of a moment,
until it becomes a memory*

*"Silence is the best answer
of all stupid questions."*

*"Smile is the best reaction
of hard situation."*

*"Walk alone until someone
is trully willing to walk with you."*

"Talk about ideas not about people"

*Everyone wants to be your friend
when you have something they want."*

*"They will put you last
and call you first when they need
something."*

"No one cares, until
you are rich, famous or dead."

"You always get tested most
before you progress
to the next level."

"The only one person I trust
is the person I see in the mirror."

Don't be angry to people
who don't have the capacity to change."

"Weak people revenge
Strong people forgive
intelligent people ignore."

"A person who is ok with being alone
is a powerful person."

"If nobody hates you
you are doing something boring."

"Never complains about the difficulties
because GOD always gives the hardest
to the best one."

*"The more I find myself
the more people I lose"*

*"Tell a lie once
and your all truth will be ignored"*

*"When people love you, they don't tell you
when people tell you, they don't love you"*

*"Pay attention to the people who don't
clap for your winning"*

"We should love, not fall in love
because everything falls get broken."

"Burn the past, turn the page
and move on"

"Never beg, never trust, never
depend on someone else."

"A strong person doesn't revenge
they let karma does their dirty job"

"Loyalty comes from heart, not money"

"God removes people in your life,
because he heard a conversation
you didn't hear."

'When someone does something wrong,
don't forget all things they did right"

"Discipline is doing what needs to do
even when you don't want to do it"

"Teach your heart to accept
disappointments, even from people
you love"

"Success is never permanent
and failure is not the end"

"You never know how strong you are
until being strong is the only choice
you have"

"Never trust your fears
they don't know your strength"

"Pain makes you stronger"

"Tears make you braver"

"Heartbreak makes you wiser"

"Thank the past for the better future"

"Failures are a part of life, if you don't fail
you don't learn, if you don't learn
you will never change"

"Knowledge will give you power,
but character will give you respect"

"If you want to make everyone happy
sell Ice cream"

"Every success story is
a tale of constant adaptation,
revision and change"

*"Habits may change but
human nature will remain".*

*"Not all storms disturb your life,
sometimes it clears your way"*

*'Don't listen to what people say
behind you, ignore it"*

*"If it wasn't hard, everyone would do it
Only the hard one makes it greats"*

*"There is no days off
when you depend on yourself"*

*"It is easy to find the new one
but it's hard to find the true one"*

*"Stop missing someone who doesn't
even think about you"*

*"Loyalty is rare
If you find it, keep it"*

"When trust is broken,
sorry means nothing"

"Be happy with what you have
while working for what you want"

Never tell people your weakness
because they will use it
to against you"

"When someone helps you
while they are struggling too
that is not a help but love"

"Keep humble spirit"

"They just want to see your reaction"

*"Don't go broke helping people
because when you broke
nobody will help you"*

*"People will say "you changed"
because they don't want to see
you grow."*

*"A clear rejection is better
than a fake promise"*

*"Maturity is when you decide to stay calm
rather than arguing"*

*"Family is not about the blood.
It is about who willing to hold your hand
when you need it the most"*

*"You call it difficulties
I call it challenges"*

*"Who you need is only yourself,
make your dream happens"*

"Be the player not the audience"

*"People bring up your past,
when they are intimidated by your
presence"*

*"When you have a million dollars vision
don't surround them with 1 cent mind"*

"Rumours are carried by haters,
spread by fools and
accepted by idiots

"Happiest people are the givers
not the takers"

"Don't be ashamed of your
work or hustle. nobody will feed you
if you go broke"

"Your attitude more important
than your degree"

Don't judge people from their choice
they made when you don't know
the options they had"

"Most people loyal to their needs only
not to you"

"Stop overthinking
you just make your problem bigger"

"What they can"t see
they can't ruin it"

"You can be so important to someone
but only when it is for their benefit"

"The real you are, the smaller
your circle will be"

"Don't sit at the table where they talk about
other, because when you get up, you will be
the next topic"

"Sometimes giving someone second
chance is like giving them second bullet
to shoot you again"

"I'm not what happened to me
but I am what I choose
to become"

"Less curious about people
and more curious about ideas"

"The root of joy is gratefullness"

"Once you have accepted your flaws,
no one can use them to against you"

*"My energy will always match yours,
so, when my energy is off, check yours"*

*"Once you can be grateful for any condition,
healing begins"*

"Heal your body with your thoughts"

*"Those who lack the courage to take a challenges
will always find reasons to cover"*

"Don't forget the hands that raised you"

"No matter how busy you are,
if you really care you will always
find time for someone"

"Destroy the old you, before
it destroys you"

"If I walk by myself,
at least I know I am with someone
I can trust"

"It's better to be unhappy and
know the worst than to be happy
in fool's paradise"

"People these days gain attention
by losing respect"

"Learn to say NO without explaining"

"Some days I can't stop thinking about you,
but the other days I wonder
why I am wasting my time"

*"You want to grow?
let them go"*

*"It's not about the money,
It's freedom"*

*"Let it hurt
until it can't hurt anymore"*

"Stop watering a dead flower"

"A fake smile can fool a crowd of people,
but it can not heal the pain"

"In order to win,
you must understand the game"

"Some people in your family will
come miles to bury you but won't even cross
the street to support when
you're still alive"

"Remember, everyone is only sweet when
they first meet,
a fisherman only gives the best bait
before the fish is caught"

*"If you never taste a bad apple
you will not appreciate a good apple
you must have life experience
to undestand life"*

"Life is a gift, use it wisely"

*"Play smart, act like you
didn't notice anything"*

*"Trust, takes years to build
seconds to break and
forever to repair"*

*"Life goes on
So don't waste your time
worrying about your mistake"*

"Pain in my heart but smile in my face"

*"If they are okay with losing you,
stop fighting"*

"Only memories will last forever"

"'You can not be wise and in love
at the same time"

"Your friends are a reflection of your own
personality, the smarter you are
the more selective you become"

"Win it in silence"

"Stop caring and they will stop hurting"

*"Forget about how much it will hurt,
and go for it"*

*"LISTEN and SILENT are spelled
with same letters.
Think about it"*

*"love yourself first because it is
the only one who will accompany you
for the rest of your life"*

*"Your life is not yours
if you always care what others think"*

"one day your consistent hard work
and sacrifice will pay off"

'Discipline is explaining to your brain
that you need more sacrifice than having fun
to achieve a bright future"

"Be selective, be wise and be smart"

"True friends don't compete
they support each other"

"Make small circle"

*"Don't forget GOD
when you get what you prayed for."*

*"People will never truly understand
something, until it happens to them"*

*"Your life, your choice, your
decision"*

"Discipline is the ability to stay focused and dutiful in the face of millions distractions"

"Worrying is a waste of time, It doesn't change anything but distrurbs your mind and happiness"

"Before engaging in gossip about someone's life, remember that there are chapters of your life you don't want to read aloud either"

"Never over react, stay in control"

"Stop making yourself easily available
for people who never prioritized
you"

Maturity ia learning when to
walk away from people and situation
that threaten your pecae of mind, value
and self worth"

"NOTHING is forever, be humble"

"When nobody stands for you
That is the time you have to stand
for yourself"

"People are prisoners of their phone
that is why it is called "cell phone""

"Don't let negative thoughts
destroys you"

"When GOD is silent,
He is preparing something great
for you"

"Never eat the last piece of something
you didn't buy

"Be your own light to face your darkness"

*"If prayers becomes your hobby
then miracles will become your lifestyle"*

*"Every failure has hidden lesson
to be learnt"*

*"I cried because I have no shoes
But I stopped crying when I saw a man without
leg.. Life is full of blessing, but sometimes
we don't realize it*

"Be right to others
not because they are but because you are"

"Something good will not always be right
but something right will always be good
in the end"

"the things you can not buy with money
will always be the most valuable things
in the world"

'The realest people don't have
many friends"

"Don't regret having a good heart,
everything will comeback and multiply"

"Some people are so fake
Even china denied to admit
if they made it"

"What you hide in your heart
appears in your eyes"

"Always walk in confidence
because GOD is with you"

"Don't force yourself to fit in somewhere
you don't belong"

'Be happy in front of people
who don't like you.
It kills them"

"Protect your peace at any cost"

"My resilience level is so high
even my problem needs a coffee break"

"Stop setting yourself on fire for people
who will just sit there and watch you burn"

"When life gets hard, don't wish it to be
easier, decide to be stronger"

"I went through my darkest time alone,
that is why I act like
I don't need anyone"

"Don't quit !
Life can go from zero to hundred
in a real quick"

""Strength doesn't come from what
you can do. Strength comes from things
you once thought you couldn't do.""

"What comes easy won't last long
and what last long won't come
easy"

"Don't blame the clown for acting like
a clown, but ask yourself why
you keep going to the circus"

"Difficult doesn't mean Impossible"

"Winners are not those who never fail,
but those who never quit"

"Don't limit your challenges
but challenge you limits"

"Be careful who you trust
even sugar and salt look the same"

"Sit at the table where they are
talking about growth and goals
not other people"

"No one will ever know how much pain
it took to be this calm"

"Don't live your life with anger and hate
you will be hurting yourself
only"

"Worrying doesn't take away
tomorrow's problem. It will take
your peace away"

"Your future depends on
what you do now"

"as bad as you want to address it,
It is the best to let GOD defend you.
He saw too."

"Move in silence
only speak when it is time to say
"checkmate""

"People's quality can be known from
what topics they talk about"

"you can't defeat a man
who doesn't care about pain, rejection
failure, loss, disrespect and heartbreak.
he is here to win"

*"Life becomes easier when you learn
to accept an apology
you never got"*

*"Happiness is found on the way,
not at the end of the road"*

*"People who shine from within
don't need the spotlight"*

*"Confuse them with you silence
and amaze them with your result"*

*"The smarter you get
the less you speak"*

*"The truth doesn't cost anything
but a lie can cost you everything.*

*"Forgiving doesn't make you weak
it sets you free"*

*"People are like books,
some deceive you by its cover
and other surprise you by its content"*

"Don't let the ugly in others
kill the beauty in you"

"Once you fall in love with yourself
their game is over"

'It is heart of gold and stardust soul
that makes you beautiful"

"You must be stronger than your feelings"

*"The universe is not trying to break you
It's trying to wake you up so that you'll see
what is the real and worth fighting for"*

*"Your value doesn't decrease
based on someone's inability
to see your worth"*

*"Don't look back, you are not going
that way"*

*"The wrong one will find you in peace
and leave you in pieces"*

"The right one will find you in pieces
and lead you to peace"

"Do the work others are not willing to do
and you will get the things
others will never have"

"If you have power to go alone
in restaurant / cinema hall, then
you can do everything in your life"

"If they want to leave,
hold the door open for them"

"Mindset is everything"

"Life is too short to tolerate non sense"

*"If you need new response
just stay away from them"*

*"Don't blame the distractions,
Improve your focus and discipline"*

"Tell my mistakes to me not others
because it will be corrected by me
not others"

"Always be ready to survive alone
today you are important to them
tomorrow you are nothing to them"

"There is no partner in this world
who can replace parental love"

"Negativity may come knocking at your door
but it doesn't mean you have to
let it in"

*"If you want to know how rich you are
count the things you have
that money can not buy"*

*"The tongue has no bones
but it strong enough to break a heart"*

*"You are bigger than
what is making you anxious"*

*"Never beg for a seat
when you can build your own table"*

*"Do good they will talk, do bad they will talk
so do whatever you need and
let them talk"*

*"When you entertain a clown
you become a part of the circus"*

*"Everyday is new beginning
to make today better than yesterday"*

*"The pain will leave
once it has finished teaching you"*

"Don't be afraid to start over again,
this time you are not starting from scratch
you are starting from experinces"

"Learn to speak only things
that are necessary and useful.
Otherwise, keep quiet"

"Never give up on the person,
you want to become"

"Problems are never too big
we just overthink about it"

*"Everyone will leave
but God will always stay with me"*

*"Learn to be grateful,
live your life with what you have"*

*"Their opinions say nothing
about your value"*

*Äs long as you don't give up
nothing is over"*

*"Surround yourself with people
who know your worth"*

*I'm not negotiating my value
with anyone"*

*"If I change, it's because I want to,
not because of other people"*

*"Yourself worth is not define
by the way people treat you"*

*"The only thing you can do about awful people,
don't be one of them"*

*"If you don't call me , I understand
If you don't text me, I understand
and when I forget you
I hope you understand"*

*'A single dream is more powerful
than thousand realities"*

*"I don't work for money
I work for freedom"*

"Trust what you feel not what you hear"

*"Never ignore a person who cares for you
because someday you will realize that
you have lost a diamond when you were busy
collecting stones"*

"Love people from a save distance"

*"You were born empty-handed
God provided you with brain"*

*"Stop trying calm the storm.
Calm yourself, the storm will pass"*

"Enjoy simple things in life"

*"Sit with the winners,
the conversation will be different"*

*"Never hide your bad side to make
someone stay. Show your bad side
and see who will stay"*

*"Never argue with idiots,
They will drag you to their level"*

*"Some people talk about you
because they lost their privilege
to talk to you"*

*"You lose nothing when you leave
fake people"*

*"When you are dead, you don't know
you are dead. It is only painful for others.
The same applies when you are stupid"*

"Do what scares you until it doesn't"

*"Avoid people who act like a victim
in the problem they created"*

*"Nobody can make you happy
if you are not happy inside"*

"You will get what you gave"

*"The most dangerous liars
are those who think they are telling
the truth"*

*"People only treat you
the way you allow them to treat you.
Be free"*

"Be cool not cold"

"Stay away from what broke you"

"When you start to improve yourself
loneliness is the price you must pay"

"The broken one will always be
able to love harder than most because
once you have been in the dark, you learn
to appreciate everything that shines"

"Don't make someone who doesn't even
care about you become your
priority"

"Forgive them even when they are not sorry
Let them be right, if that's what they need.
don't tie yourself to small-mindedness"

*"If you can not see the light,
Then be the light"*

*"Your biggest fan is a stranger
your biggest hater is someone
you know"*

*"The biggest asset in the world
is your mindset"*

*"Trust is built on telling the truth
not what they want to hear"*

*"Being broke is a part of the journey,
staying broke is a choice"*

*"Sometimes we need to remove people
without warning. Don't waste your time
explaining what they already know
they were doing wrong"*

*"If you can not control what you think
you can not control what you do"*

*"More people would learn from their mistake
if they weren't so busy denying them"*

*"If you have been hurt many times
and you still know how to smile.
You are a strong person"*

*"Superior people are those
that modest in their speech and exceed
in their actions"*

*"Stop telling people more than
they deserve to know"*

*" I wanna see what will happen
if I don't give up"*

"have faith and fight!"

*"I'm not scared of love,
I'm scared of loving someone
while they pretend to love me"*

"Keep your heart strong"

*"If you knew how quickly people
forget the dead, you will stop impressing
them."*

"Don't be so sweet, otherwise
they will eat you"

"If your phone doesn't ring when
you're struggling, don't pick it up
when you accomplished them all and
become the winner"

'Do the right thing and
do the thing right"

"Sometimes people don't want to hear
the truth, because they don't want
their illusions are destroyed

"Always be better than yesterday"

*"I have seen crying faces in mercedes
and smiling faces on bicycles"*

*"Just because I didn't say anything
it doesn't mean I didn't notice"*

*"If you think the price of winning
is too high, just wait until you get the bill
from regret"*

*"Bravery is not absence of fear,
bravery is feeling fear and moving forward
anyway"*

*"The greatest version of you
is your discipline to achieve your goal"*

*"When it feels scary to jump in
that is exactly when you jump
otherwise you end up staying
in the same place your whole life"*

*"Build yourself silently,
Let success speak"*

"The wrong partner will set you back
financially, mentally, spiritually and
physically"

"You think you are hurting me,
but actually you just make me look at you
differently"

"Your relationship with GOD should be
your top priority because when all else
fails you, HE won't.

"Jealous people don't necessarily want
what you have, they just don't want you
to have it"

"Never lower your standard"

*"Never expect what you give,
always close your eyes when you give"*

"Mistakes are the proof you're trying"

"No risk, No story"

"Not everyone deserves to know the real you
Let them critize who they think you are"

"Don't tell me what they said about me
but tell me why were they so comfortable
to say it around you"

"Before you judge someone about
their anger, ask them about their pain"

"We are born without bringing anything
and so do we when we die. so be humble".

"Thank you GOD for blessing me
much more than I deserve"

"Everything happens for a reason,
learn from it.

"Avoiding people for peace
is self-care"

"Nothing is impossible
If you have strong mindset"

*"I don't have plan B.
I will succeed or I will die in pursuit of it"*

"Hunt or get hunted"

*"Don't stop when you're tired
but stop when you're done"*

*"Dreams are not what you see in sleep
dreams are things which do not
let you sleep"*

"If you focus on the hurt, you will continue to suffer but if you focus on the lesson you will continue to grow"

"People are being hated when they are real and being loved when they are fake"

"Actions prove who someone is and words prove who they want to be"

"There will never be a perfect time, just start from where you are"

*"Look at a pencil.
It is easy to look sharp
when you haven't done any work"*

*"Time can change black coal
to shinny diamond"*

*"It takes nothing to join the crowd
but it takes everything to stand alone"*

*"Let sleep in a clean heart
let peace surround us"*

*"Take care of your thoughts
when you are alone
and take care of your words
when you are with people"*

*"Surround yourself with those who
bring out the best in you
not the stress in you"*

*"Without direction and focus
even a genius can not achieve
anything"*

*"No one can destroy iron but its own rust can.
No one can destroy a person but his own
mindset can"*

*"Dreams without actions
is nothing"*

*"Failure and success are parts of life.
Both of them are not permanent.
So, keep fighting"*

*"Stop being afraid of what could go wrong
and being excited about what could go right"*

*"When you see something beautiful
in someone, tell them.
it will take seconds to say but
it will last a lifetime for them"*

*"Everything is very difficult
at the first time only"*

*"Look for 3 things in a person
intelligence, energy and integrity
If they don't have the last one don't even
bother with the first two"*

*"Do things for people not because
who they are but because who
you are"*

*"I see you are trying,
please, keep going"*

*"Stop expecting and start accepting
Life becomes easier"*

"Excuses can't build an empire"

*"When you grow in silence
nobody will disturb you"*

*"One day the word "soon"will be replaced
by "finally""*

"GOD's plan will always more beautiful
than our desires"

"One day you will realize
material things mean nothing"

"Never give up on your prayer
GOD always answer in
unexpected ways"

"Some things take time,
no matter how good the efforts you have
Be patient"

"Be thankful for yesterday.
Be grateful for today .
Be hopeful for tomorrow"

"When they judge you, remember this :
dogs bark when they don't recognize people"

"A fish with a closed mouth
will never get caught"

"The distance between dream and reality
is called actions.
Take bold steps, your destiny awaits"

"The harder you work for something,
the greater you will feel when you
achieve it"

"The world is changed by actions
not words"

"If the first step is very hard for you
make it becomes smaller steps"

"Life is too short for arguments,
just say "I don't care"and move on"

"a Family is the bonds we create.
The strength we found in one another
not by blood only"

"Don't judge a situation
you have never been in"

"In life, the greatest risk
is not taking one"

"Today a reader, tomorrow a leader"

*"Change is uncomfortable
but necessary"*

*"While you're busy, doubting yourself
Someone out there is admiring
your strength"*

*"A man settles when he finds peace
not money, not beauty and status"*

*"When they said "impossible"
it is for them not for you"*

*"The biggest communication problem is
we listen to reply not to understand"*

*"Don't let the bad days make
you think you have a bad life"*

*"Change is always scary
but I'm excited because I'm entering
new chapter in my life"*

*"Beauty catches attraction
but character catch heart"*

"Ïf you can not find good people
in your life, be the one"

"What you sow is what you will reap"

"Love dies because of ego"

"Take care of your parents
they are the "only one" who wants you
to be happy"

*"If you want to cry, just cry
but don't let them know.
Be strong, you can do it"*

*"I don't treat people badly
I treat people accordingly"*

*"Even if you trust someone
don't tell them everything"*

*"Just don't care what anybody else
is doing, focus on yours.
Nothing else"*

"Don't argue, accept the situation, stay away and move on"

"Be different. Don't be one of them"

"If they are trying to leave you, help them"

"Be so busy so that you don't have time to be sad"

"Sometimes distance will teach you the value of a person"

"You will always be misunderstood by those who don't want to understand you"

"Most time your enemies were once your friends"

"Life's greatest freedom which is have nothing to prove"

"If a dog can say something, maybe
it will say "I'm not the best but I have
never broken someone's heart for
temporary fun""

"Treat me like a game,
and I will teach you how to play"

"a sprinter once said
"I trained 4 years to run 9 seconds/100m.
but people give up when they don't see
result in 2 months""

"Teach your children
with what you were never taught"

"Challenges are not sent to destroy you
but to promote, increase and strengthen you."

"They hate me because it is easier
than beating me"

"You can not be strong all the time,
sometimes you just need to be alone
and let your tear out"

"This is the wrong generation
for the people who have good hearts"

"I am stuck in generation
when loyalty is just a tattoo, love is just a quote,
happiness is a myth and being fake is the
lifestyle"

'Life is the most difficult exam,
most people, they are trying to copy others
not realizing that everyone has different
question paper"

"Change how you see things,
find an opportunity to grow
and leave the rest"

'Don't be afraid to be alone
It is much better than you waste your
time with wrong partner.

"Some of generous people have no money.
Some of wisest people have no education.
Some of the kindest people were hurt
the most"

"If you prayed for it,
then no reason to worry.
When the time comes, GOD will give you
what is yours"

"This world doesn't care about your pain,
so, be strong"

"Always ask God to give direction in your life"

Dear reader,

Hopefully, this book can help you to see this world more clearly. So you can determine your future steps in life better.

Thank you for reading and If this book is useful for you, please take a moment to provide a review of this book, so that other people can also get benefit from reading this book.

Best Wishes,

Robbert Piontek